THE ISLAND IN THE SOUND

NIALL CAMPBELL

THE
ISLAND
IN THE
SOUND

BLOODAXE BOOKS

ISBN: 978 1 78037 721 6

First published 2024 by
Bloodaxe Books Ltd,
Eastburn,
South Park,
Hexham,
Northumberland NE46 1BS.

www.bloodaxebooks.com

For further information about Bloodaxe titles
please visit our website and join our mailing list
or write to the above address for a catalogue.

Supported using public funding by
**ARTS COUNCIL
ENGLAND**

Cover design: Neil Astley & Pamela Robertson-Pearce

Printed in Great Britain by Bell & Bain Limited, Glasgow, Scotland, on
acid-free paper sourced from mills with FSC chain of custody certification.

for Soren and Catriona

CONTENTS

I think that, if required on pain of death to name
instantly the most perfect thing in the universe,
I should risk my fate on a bird's egg

THOMAS WENTWORTH HIGGINSON, 1862

You do not bear the signs
Of one who's fathomed how the candle shines.

FROM *The Conference of the Birds* by FARID UD-DIN ATTAR

PART I

'I am so Happy. I am so Happy. I Loved my Life'

said Gerard Manley Hopkins as he died.
Forty-four, auraed in sweat – his nurse
a shadow by the shaking lamp. I read
this strange, this hard emphatic, *life is good*,

said at the door of nothingness; how could
the nothing not react? Those words, that voice.
At once, there was the spreading night-time desert,
all million dunes, with each part trembling at

the first soft call of thunder, when the rain
is just about to fall, like exhaled breath.
Oh voice. The Land of Death laid out and washed –
and brought to something else. Utterly different.
Oh words. That pull us to the autumn forest
instead, this place of rain, and changes us.

Apprenticeship

Dusk on the water, the job was to watch,
unracked, the wet still-dripping creels being tipped
into the grading tray, alive with life.

Our seas provided black-eyed velvet crabs
with small horns ridging their top plates. The work:
to grade by size, *Those big as a fist*, they pointed –

Big as a heart, I saw – were lifted out
as worth a better price. Hours, you would weigh
by hand and eye and a slow part of the mind,

young jeweller at a tray of breathing stones;
arbiter at the filling, refilling box.
The night progressing until the shed light

drew out thick moths. To work was to find yourself
drawn in – or was it drawn back – to something
careful and mysterious, hard-shelled and resistant.

Big as a fist or heart. The same rain falls
on that shed and on this house. I did it five years,
and then did it for the rest of my life.

Island Sonnets: Fugay

Bee island. Hive holed in the beach,
their private store of lick-sweet honey
combing strangely in the grit.
Sea-flowers' hexagon, part sugar

part salt, are gathered and then set.
Scarcity means it all is brought:
primrose nectar, campion,
pink thrift, the nectar of the rock

opening in the surf. Tight flavours
of this half-mile, this closed taste-map.

There are two ways, that I have seen,
to be present. The swelling queen
quivers like a just struck match. Nearby
our basking shark steers through its dark.

The Sparrow's Legs

These thin   /   /   hold up the sparrow
as if a little hymn to Kierkegaard
Either/Or   Either/Or   they seem to say
damp, wet fog   cotton of the morning

or mimic the mosquito stem   /   /
that dips, twice, into the world's arm
through mulch ground   through soil, dark skin
draw of seed and spore   the worm path veins

or stylus pressed to the day's record   /   /
with net thread; wool strand; book lent against the wind.
Various and plain – they seem hopeful,
the way they slant   /   /   like two thin pens

as if the love letter were being written
at the exact same moment as the letter's reply.

The Night Birds

The whole deep drawer would be emptied –
with each sock singled and then rolled
into a sort of fabric cannonball

or enlarged lead-shot, light in the hand;
these would be lined up close-by one – me, maybe,
or my brother, sometimes my mother or father.

This person was gunman in the stiff dawn.
Everyone else was a bird – a *Sgarbh* –
who were to ball up on the ground, almost nesting,

the reed-land of the night-time kitchen,
body tucked in tight over the knees.
The game was for the birds to lift up, flying,

still knelt, but in a kind of upright, flapping cross.
Cawing and calling – boasting they were alive.
The gunman was to try to shoot them down.

All night, we swapped roles, becoming both
the long arm's gun, the chest's downed target.
Still young, we'd held no other life

but this first time we tasted variousness:
each a gunman fallen into armistice,
with all shots blown; a gunman with a row

of laid-out wings; a bird brought silent
in the middle of their calling;
or the last bird, momentarily triumphant,
who did not find their triumph end.

Inside the Trojan Horse: A War Poem

Some in their lives before had raised horses –
and touched the belly of the mare
so knew how thin the wall that separated
the land of breath from where young horse
lay, wet-legged, in its soul's field.

Soldiers in this shuttered cabin,
each was surprised to find a new thorn rising
from what to them had been the placid but astonishing,
the foal remembered newborn, head bowed
and waiting, as if for the wound of the reins.

Tongues of Water

We went each Sunday for the mass
recited in my parent's language
that wasn't mine. The Gaelic gospel

that was just sound, pure sound, to me.
I rose and kneeled, and listened as
my people traded vowel for vowel;

my whole small world, this flowing water.
Back then, I sat and heard the ocean
in their unknowable call,

that same unknowable response.
My parents stood in the psalm's current
like waders gone out, as I settled

knee-deep on a second bank,
hearing only the sound of a stream,
believing only the sound the stream makes.

Dear,

It feels like we're between two moments,
the summer's over, winter coming,
promising all its fireworks
to the night sky near our two rivers;
it doesn't seem long ago, remember,
taking the taxi to the restaurant
but asking to be let out early
near our first house. I proposed, then,
in the rain, beneath the umbrella,
on the stone bench near the medical building.
Not the start of love but the start
of marriage –
                maybe it is always
like this: the sense of being housed
someway out in the drift. And now
away from the beginning, facing
the sense that things not at the start
feel like they are drawing to their end;
love – as well as this whole era:
counselled, comfortable years of building
in the sand. You know my thoughts,
I don't think the world can last long,
doom-monger, pessimist, and man
who made a promise in the rain,
sat on the blanket, on the stone –
I hold to the idea that things
do fall apart but despite this
there is still time for respite love.

Wet hair in the restaurant, we drank wine
and took turns to phone our friends,
the food arriving on huge plates.
The more is taken, the more eagerly they devote themselves,
and filling the cells, and building their stores from flowers...
Virgil wrote about his bees:
not long after the death of Caesar,
some time before the fall of Rome.

After the Language Deprivation Experiment

(for Paul Auster)

I had never seen such paleness,
the cold breeze pouring through his body,
outside our walled town, the wet autumn
cidering the last unpicked apples
locked to their branch. One horseman leading
the group across the mossed bog-grounds:
the retinue of the mute nurse,
the tall, gagged soldiers, guarding language.

Fredrick II and James IV tried this,
Herodotus found in Egypt
some attempt was made – but it took a country
like our own to see it right.
Brown hills, deep lochs, land of long winters.
We made our way in the boy's wake;
the full moon of his head, his forearms
implying bones as thin as ice
around a ghost apple,
his whole black eyes. We wondered if
beneath his robes he might have earned
a pair of closed, arthritic wings
against the spine, a mirrored harp
all gut and string, and never played.

Our tiny hope and prisoner,
newborn, we brought him screaming to his room
still pink and raw
and swaddled in his birthing colours,
before the first *shhhhh* and comfort,
or first song whispered at his ear.

The treatise: deprived of all our words,
his mother singing by the sink,
the open books, the radio,
the billboard at the motorway,
that he, like a stranger in a forest,
would come to something of that first tongue
that Adam taught himself in Eden:
the clean, clear lexicon he tasted
right at the source, right from the god-well.

For years, we watched him growing,
uneasy with his change,
his small beaked mouth, his withered tongue,
his jabbering when the stretched sky
dropped red with sunset or blood sunrise –
one time, a snowfall set him howling
but with such beauty and such music
that I almost pulled down my gag
and called to him. But never did.

Our soft anticipation fell
like chaff, and in the below field
workers moved in their machinery,
our small caravan came to the cliff
and its erected stage.
                              Birds yelled and dived
into the blue depths. On my turn
to shuffle past and hear him speak
I had already seen the men
and women leaving, each one weeping.
Up close, brought before the boy,
I saw the sores erupt his skin,

his thin life swaying, his harelip,
delicate as if painted on,
and father to my own hurt boy
I mumbled my apology,
reaching for his hand, I kissed him,
for all that I had brought him to.

Then, beyond each other,
struggling like all fathers with their sons,
his black eyes staring at the water
gone white with surf, he spoke
and I heard smoke folding, white ribbon
on white ribbon, and I didn't know;
and I heard the quail of mice
inside the tree, the shout of fog,
the name of snow, and didn't know,
and didn't know, and couldn't understand.

A Man Carrying His Own Door

Ah yes, the man is at his life again.
Or so I think – when watching him,
prince with his duties, easing nails
from a hinge, the hinge from its grooved wall.

He liked this work. The hammer stroke,
the chisel peeling butter curls
of whitest wood – their pattern fall
around the job's circumference.

And now it's lifted free – hauled free
into the air – just like those tenants,
who, once evicted, since wood was rare,
were free to take their doors with them.

Can't you see it? The huge shield-weight
of a door being carried by a man.
Near seventy, now. But just you try
to share the weight, or take an end.

Oblivion – or something softer
and just as dark has said its name.
The rain is knocking, hard as light,
where he holds the wood beside his ear.

Life of the Night Auditor

(The 11pm-7am Shift)

And as they explained everything: the bright screen,
        the rows, the columns and their tallying,
        the closed accounts of all the sleeping rooms,
        and then the final line brought into balancing,

I heard something familiar, and then
        a second familiar thing: remembering
        the tale of a man set to work in the king's field
        with a white sheet and a black pen, scribbling

the full inventory of the geese roosting on the field's floor;
        the snipe, bog-bedded; moon in the frame of the lake;
        feeling, after the terror, that locked-in
        privateness come from looking at the dark.

I saw the turn of the last car – and then heard the soft engine
        of the day's first bus beginning its lift.
        Those nights the same as the tale's life, one of those,
        gloom-muddied, dawn-dusted, who sleep in the light.

Hamelin

I played and started with a little thing
I played the fox's eyes inside the den

I played the fool and did the fool's dance
I played the echoes of the underpass

I played until the night rose, the moon fell
I played the sugar's melt to caramel

I played the field, its sunflower patch
I played with danger in the safety match

I played, it was a slap and a harder kiss
I played, in part, to fill the silences

I played against myself in a shadow-match
I played the cloud-form of the cataracts

I played at cards, at chess, at tic-tac-toe
I played the atom and its afterglow

I played all the good luck, all the bad luck
I played at whisky in the coffee cup

I played, one time, the rats into the stream,
I played, do you follow me, or not follow me?

Morning Lessons

Cold Sunday in the school's tarred playground –
the flat course round the shuttered classrooms

and mute bells. I was out of breath,
running and running – balancing

what he couldn't balance yet: the speeding,
moving bicycle. Its blood-like frame.

Keep going, keep going, I kept saying,
as his legs whirled their small, aired nothings.

Everything, then, seemed a short road
towards new manhood, adulthood.

Weaving directionless, but here
and there, he started to guide straight.

Time's rain fell on me, when he steadied
and pushed off, as if from my hands;

I was still running forwards – even
when I shouted to be left behind.

Three Folk-tale Characters Who Are Definitely Not Metaphors for the Poem

Maria

Who saw the landowner at his own business
and who wouldn't see again. Who had fresh earth
and a white seed packed into the two small plots
where her eyes had been. Maria, who was saddest
through that initial winter – but who felt that first
strong pull of spring opening out of her
as two green stems. Who was to know
the shortest roots belong to mint.
The third summer, she wore the thick stems
like a green bandage. Who was to flower
all through her wedding month, and who,
eyes filled up with earth, was said to see the first steps
the dying make in the land of the dead.

Ferguson

Who found the sea-tributes at his door:
clam piles, fuzz-haired mussels, a weed crown
that if you wore, you'd hear the far-off rain
on its way to shore. But who stepped over them
on his way inside. Last of our seal catchers,
and seal skinners, last of the skin tailors
whose hands could turn out gloves
like slips of oil. Who did not mind
the thinning of their stock – who should have stopped
at the first mark of water on his house-step.
Who came home, after, to no seal gifts
but to the little ribbon of a stream
winding through his house, the pale sand
through the hall, the neat arrangement
of his children's clothes on their beds,
as though basking, each on a ledge of rock,
emptied, as by a knife or by the moonlight.

Whose own grandmother tried herself to starve
because she feared his mouth. Who was stowed
in the locking barn, but who ate the straw
and wickering; who ate the rope and found
the honey in its knot, bit down the crackle-trim
of the soil trough; who ate his own mother
through the womb, or so the slander went.
Who found a mouth for brass, a tongue for iron
and a tooth to chew the hard stuff down.
Who came out new-forked at the world's plate.
Eating the cherries. Finding house bulbs *in season*.
Who rattled like a coin box when he danced.

Island Sonnets: Delos

I see the island's inadvertent grace:
Delos, Apollo's home of the pale shore

and black geese. The sacred Mediterranean
where none were allowed to die or to be born.

My mother nurses her own brother through
his end, moving from kitchen to his room

with those hot cloths, their white folds in her hand.
Dying seems this constant needing to be cleaned.

Long nights of cotton brushing skin. I see
what they were saved, when birth was just a wrapped child

handled onto land – and death's coffin-walk
was the still-living led to the shore's end.

All the hands waving to them. Back and forth.
The same movement of my mother as she tends.

The Death of the Birds

Tonight, the blue Book of the Universe
falls open on the page, The Death of the Birds;
holding descriptions of grass-chaliced, mud-set nestings
gone cold, of dwindling Vs heading northwards.
There are captions about the rot in the colony,
when the whole flock washed in, like the worst tide.
They said, they'll say: it all came unannounced.
Already, plain speckled eggs were imagined eucharistic
in the twig's brown bowl. The loss circled;
silence above all silence called out over the evening fields.

They Have Crept Down,

so out of place; to graze the street's black field.
Vague silhouettes in the burnt streetlights,
still noticeably furred, brown and delicate,

their eyes still large; they move, acclimatised
to the lifting *tut* of their hooves on tarred road.
Once, coming home late in November,

I turned our corner to see a deer resting
on the wet bed of the pavement –
it was ghostly, but shared all the sad wonder

of a thing being where it shouldn't:
I saw a drowned book on the beach, or a pile
of discarded clothes, unreadable in the snow.

The rowan scatters berries
throughout the forest, a mile from our home.
The firs hang the fog from their branches.

Strange meetings. The wild deer and myself.
We stopped on this cold road that led past grace;
they licked the moisture from the parked car's headlights.

Barn Owl on Newburgh Road

If breath was any animal, it's this.
Glide and hush-sweep
across the close-by fields of grain.

White, blank faces. They aren't wisdom
and aren't talk;
they are the breath of someone sleeping.

The slow intake of the night air
as the wing rises,
the down-beat of my wife's chest as it sinks.

Dear,

I have been drinking through the afternoon
but felt that I wanted to write you;
we sat in the café by the station
and watched as the young people passed –
and I wondered who wrote this youth best:
pale, trembling in their bright colours,
the strange wound of youth –
do you remember how bad we were at it,
being young, I mean:
wine drinkers in the student kitchen
while the party happened around us.
You telling me how, *you know,*
the cabinet of curiosity is the perfect form
while I nodded like a drunk man in love,
teeth and lips black –
it seemed in these art forms, you place
an array of small things together:
a tooth, a comb, a blue ribbon,
the centremost of those Russian dolls,
and maybe, like this, they will speak to each other;
maybe, like this, something opens,
like a shelf of books all opening at once.
You wore pearl earrings, I remember that
and I had a brown suit jacket
and since there were no wine glasses, we drank from mugs;
all these small things happened
just there, just then, and just like that.

A Car for Jacob

Here, let me lay its four wheels down
on this first country and first road,
pioneer way of linoleum.
Brakeless, gearless, it must steer
under the deft weight of the palm;
its pull-back-and-go, arrow-like,
notched – flown – the bow, invisible.

Ancient toy horses were discovered
in Japan. Wooden and cut-reined.
Lovingly careworn. Attesting
how all our first dreams are of moving.
Born with a clear map and a blank page,
young rider, head on. Young driver, mark
down that first ribbon of the road.

Island Sonnets: Eriskay

Today, in the field's breath,
I found where night sleeps through the daylight:

the spade cut through the furtive, rooted, inkiness,
until a wettish dark was removed and laid out.

We dug beneath bog cotton and day's butterwort,
revealing past the sundew and wild moss

into something richly fragrant. Discovery is
an action of the heart – and we went deep

or so I remember it, now on the night walk,
as every breath brings back broken top-ground,

mud hands, the aliveness of the moving body,
the aliveness of the ear pressed to the earth,

hearing the buried lateness just stirred awake;
the smell of smoke's hour, before any candle's lit.

The Cockle-picker

He lifts the notch of shell, small cup,
our thimble of the sea's champagne,
our muscle drink, the flesh-downed taste.
Worlds off from wine, and what wine toasts.

Low tide, the beckon clouds all out,
the cockle shells raked fresh; hands prising
their groove-cut, pearl-white cask. He savours,
same as I do, this coastal life.

The Salmon of All Knowledge

(for Ian Duhig)

> Fionn mac Cumhaill caught and then began to cook
> the salmon of all knowledge
>
> CELTIC MYTHS AND LEGENDS

All night I ate the perfect meal
that lifted from its bones
and waited like a famished scholar
for what I soon would know:

the movements of the stationed moon,
the languages of Spain,
the pull and billow of the heart
and rigging of its veins;

I was quite ready to go off
and raise a violin
discovering my songbook filled,
like rainfall fills a stream;

I'd know just where the gold was hidden,
vaulted in the hill,
the hidden password to the love
of every hometown girl.

But when I set my fork aside
and pushed away my plate,
I found whatever I was promised
had failed to find its place

and worse than this, I drew a blank
on all the things I'd known;
my life was just a snow-white page
nailed up onto a door;

what kindnesses I'd earned or shown,
the routes I knew for home,
my rivalries and hated men,
had left for other towns.

So, standing there, I was a rock,
a rose-hedge in the snow,
I was a tree full with the fruit
of all I didn't know –

and what was strange, joined with the fear
there was a kind of peace –
that I had shirked my other life,
its nametag and its noose;

and there, beside my empty plate,
was free to start afresh;
though hard to tell if this is different
and altered from the first,

there were no books of history
no teacher at the desk,
no pen, no ink, no copied rules,
no priest in snowy vestments,

since there, the start of knowledge was
night's blackbird in the dark;
lone singer, wearing the star's bright coat.
This was first thing that I learned.

The Islander as a Theatre Barman, Before the Ballet

Sometimes, first watcher in the upper circle,
I joined an audience of raised-up seats
to watch the ballet dancers warming up.

Their marvelled, muscled elegance. Before
the music started, they would lift each other,
all tensed frames – freed, as I saw it, from art.

So that there in the first-row dark, I thought
of those strange cousins of their act: back home,
an arm's strength being used against a rope,

fighting the sea's weight, or an uncle raising
the peat-sacks to the tractor's shelf, chest flexed,
hauling some resisting part of the earth.

But there, with rows and stalls, with balconies
of private seats – with patrons drawing close –
I sat between the shades of two knowings:

my neighbours who knew strength as an axe swung
a spade dug, a rock thrown – then, these new guides,
taut, tune-less, who used their strength to dance.

An Afterlife of Those Who Build

For some, it is a night through which they're working
the wooden, fresh, end-curve of heaven. Planning

the roof and stairs, the joists and crossbeam's position.
Paradise of a house-shell or rich ruin;

all time now just a wall on which to hoist a ladder.
I see them, the light hammer of their labour,

the light nails fixing, and since it's not all action,
I see the pause to let the plaster harden,

and the paint dry. *Now comes the time of rest,*
the old prayers say – and so for breath

they sit at the window and stare on out
into heaven's night, its moths and moon and bats,

and there, as in life, they know the thrill of catching,
surprised, a night deer come eat the fresh grass in the garden.

The Flesh Tree

Most Scottish of beliefs: a brown-green bark
shielding a bole of purest flesh;
the circlets of its bone rings rippling
through length and ledger of the trunk.

Even describing it sets the mind's fire
and brings the griddle to the heat;
shame me all you want, levering it down,
I'd scatter the snow's salt – and cook.

The tongue gives back twofold for what it tastes.
Kissed by the hot, forbidden branch,
can you imagine how the mouth might work?
You might say you wouldn't, but you would.

Island Sonnets: Sandy Island

Erewhon, in other tongues. Samuel Butler's homeland; the only source of Phostlite, Xirang, where Octiron can be mined. Mentioned first in Aeschylus's *The Lion*. Here, the spotters

come to see the last   mating pairs of
Cinnamon Birds,   nested, singing beyond
the credible.   Inkvine gardens.
Madagascar   Trees found the soil
right and   thrived. The one
country where   culture is rightfully
regarded; Isle   of no army. Isle of
the Concert   Hall where
Sibelius's 8th   Symphony
premiered its   melody of smoke;
our library   keeps the only
known copy of   Strindberg's The
Bleeding Hand   under glass. Home of
peace. Home of   the artist's restful night.
Awoken from your   sleep, it is where your

parents call from, ringing through the quiet house – on those times you can't quite reach the phone before the ringing stops.

Theology

I would explain the soul like this:
as whisky in the barrel cask –
that light caught. Grained, proofed, stored and kept
bound in a dark in wonderment;

a swilling ocean inside its drum.
Sometimes, at night, I'm left with questions:
What grain was grown, what water poured?
And, after this time, what hand gathered?

Dear,

In his best letters Van Gogh signs off with
I shake your hand.
      Isn't this perfect?
Apparently a traditional sign off, but still.
Other times he ends them: *a handshake*
or a handshake in thought. Which aren't the same.
Lacking the definitive action – the trust
that the ink can carry it.
      I bought his letters
from that second-hand bookshop in Glasgow,
the one by the fruit-shop and the bridge –
reading them on our collapsed sofa-bed
the one we covered in blankets to hide the tears;
I shake your hand.
      I don't know, but sometimes now
there's distance, much more than there was –
the sea grows, tenderness is there
but the drift's there too.
Maybe this is a later part of love,
or something more to do with age than love.
We've left Glasgow, that house, that youth
and that closeness behind with it.
We are somewhere else, parents now,
and quietly older – and from here, despite
it all, I want to write: *I kiss you* –
with its romance and its sadness and its trusting.
I'm unsure if there's anything else.

The Cured

Dughall Mac Tharmaid got the post office 1938... was not
being in the best of health, suffering from King's Fever.
This was a sickness cured only by the healing power of a
seventh son whose father was also a seventh son...

ANGUS EDWARD MACINNES, *Eriskay Where I Was Born*

His body didn't smell of earth or soil-work
or the seedlings pressed like penny moons
into the wet spring stretch. He smelt of air,
of a breeze rolled beneath a bridge,
or the world covered, hill to hill, with a veil
of frost. At night he'd leave his door

open for our bribes or gifts. Midnight's moon,
the present of a hen, slung like a bridge
across a shaking forearm, the skinned veil
forming on the milk pail. Foods that he adored.
The illness was everywhere: where we worked,
in our homes, where we slept and in the air;

it caused us to mix up dreams and life, veil-like
it kept on shifting. In the cold December air,
my friend and I sat in the doorless
wreck of on old car and went to work
naming our twelve angels. Waving at the moon
with the boy who last year had drowned at the bridge.

Later, I was certain I'd married: wide church doors
pouring out their doves, the white veil,
the bride and dress. Under a sad moon
I woke back in my house, its quiet air,
the bed and bedroom, lonely as a bridge.
It was a loss. All next day I worked

knowing I'd go to him through the fogged night air.
I think it was a dream but I crossed bridge
after bridge after bridge to his wide door,
its yellowed porchlight flickering, barely worked,
and him there, proud and stern, his veiled
threats about the cost. I paid a hundred moons

in a black purse – but as he set about to work,
I saw his blandness and knew I'd miss the badged moon,
its trail of talking, singing geese, its veil
of rain, spun out like silk. All else I give abridged,
within a year everyone had passed through his door
of sameness. And so, I saw what type of heir

the poet is: the stranger pacing on a bridge;
a dreamer, lost; the layabout, who, when everyone will work
the earth, through spite or love, will start to work the air.

Pastimes

(after Laforgue)

Ah yes, the moon! All my thoughts go to it,
and I don't think this can be changed,

pale and still – it could be dead – or is it sleeping,
guided there by the starlight's atmosphere,

all brightening circle, an O, like those windows
flowering on our silent basilicas,

it stays what it always is – perfectly there –
and I stay at a distance, watching and breathless;

its shape and curve – suddenly intimate –
that I want to bring my lips to…

another evening of this and every other thought
will run off wild and helter-skeltering

wanting no part in my thinking,
mistaking this strange and blissful moment:

me saying *Regina of the Lilies* – meaning paleness,
meaning moon – me saying *salve*,

meaning *her*, meaning the whole bright thing,
the desire to be a moth in the air.

Island Sonnets: Lingay

I think of her, our grazing island
settled only for the grass,
the sheep-boats bringing mouth and mouth,
all wild thing eaten at their stalk;

no mint, no lavender, the groove
green world sits mid-point between wildness
and farmyard. Blade-chewed paradise,
found pasture; there, its rooting mind

must turn away from its stubbed grounds,
this trample path for the whole flock,
and dream instead of long, green grasses,
wet and lying flat, uncut.
Its abandoning abandonment.
A privateness we each might want.

Learning to Drink Seawater

The fishing market drawing to a close,
the oilskins slick and wet, moon bathed in oil,

the Spanish truck ticked loudly by the shed,
and boredom surfacing – or was it triumph

calling in a small voice? – whatever it was,
we knew the taste enough, the spitting flavour,

salt-wash and weed and tin, burnt acrid silver;
but there the competition was how much

each man could drink. Tell me, can you see them,
my working, grey-haired neighbours, bending down;

their filled cup at the pier end by the boats,
older hands holding an old cup, rim chipped,

the logo a pale ghost on the porcelain;
one part brave and one part ridiculous,

it seems now an act the same as war or love:
men at the edge of what they knew, arguing:

hand me the cup, I can stand a whole mouthful –
no – I'll fill the cup, and drain it all.

Lighthouse Keeper, Believing

We steer the light that steers the voyage,
this is what I believe. Serving
to help the coal ships pass,
guiding those ships with hulls of cotton,
compartments of baled tobacco.

We stand apart, and clean the lens,
dutied – ministered – devout –
checking that the mechanism turns
and shows the rocks, and water path.

Some fail to see the work. To them
I say, you'll know us by our absence,
waking in the morning to a whole blue sky,
your wreckage of gold in the surf.

The Gift

Son, let your mother teach all other words,
I only give you: *damn*. Its one-word song,
its grief and stunned joy, its private lexicon.
Whisper it or, hurt, shout and set the birds

to the four winds. I called its breaking name
both times, when my friend died – and you were born.
Life's words, it's yours. For the kiss; for the urn
gone filled. *Damn*. Say it. Stand. Begin again.

PART II

Life Mask of William Blake

Discovered as a bald king or the soul's egg,

duck-white, a nest-warmth retained, he survives death

and comes now as a second head down the river

to where you are at the stream's bank at Glen Heather

surprised to be remembering his winter

face; those shut eyes, experiencing wonder

or some pain, that still seem ripe to open

and take you in. His snowfield jawline sloping

to the line and clear lesson of this mask,

not stopped, he only pauses for the act.

We hold this marble bell between its ringing;

but know, the hardest part is re-beginning.

The Harpy of Rubha Meall Nan Caorach

I conjure, almost tenderly,
the soaked black rocks rowed like dark lanterns
on the west beach. The ankle shallows,
stiff bladderwrack in its inch pond,
swaying with its spit of foam.

Men take in the sheep on the hill.
It rains.

       And conjure, too, the cave tunnel,
rich fetid smell of clay and straw,
like midnight in the midnight barn,
its humid gloom. My arrival.
My hands filled with a knot of bread,
new berries caught in a green bowl,
tinned peaches in a rust cylinder
from the last ship that ever came.

I conjure, from a place of turned water,
her grey wreath of hair, her sickle claws,
the tea map of her ancient skin,
and how the wings shed out beneath
the hollow of the shoulder-bone.

By that time, all she did was sit
and mouth at song. Our human bird,
feathered, balding; her, of our mixed nature.
Yes, like those who tore at Jason, spilling
the table;
       but his greatest lie was that
they only spat and shrieked – when really
she had a voice the same as ours,

but what moved it was a bird's mind;
a sparrow on the spill of grain,
a blackbird, hidden in the apples,
an osprey hung above the tide.

And what set her singing at the end
was only: dusk, pale dawn, and ice's page
on the still water, and once, when slipping,
I sliced my hand and my blood ran.

I conjure the sounds of the ocean
and her swallowing, rumours
of autumn, my own far-off name
being called and called, the sound of planes.

I conjure my own divided self, acknowledging
her two-partedness: how her head tilted back
on the hard rocks above the vineyards
when the red grapes came in – her praise,
her high poetry of licking salt
from stolen bread, excited by
the flames and smoke that rose from Crete
or settled over Lindisfarne.
I stayed because I felt a similar fissure
running through my own frame,
this time, between the flesh and the ghost.

She was at her end when I came –
so let me conjure three last things:
                                    her final morning,
hard sunlight bright enough to scar
the eyes, the body of a seal
engorged to bloating in the sands
with three wrecked boats, the church bell

ringing as though there was a fire
in the house of the world.

                                    And how,
I buried her how you might a blackbird:
an open nest of ground – closed shut,
spade by spade, until she was nestled
in the egg-like chamber of the soil.

And conjure – the sea breeze tasting
of gunshot, grain, yesterday's flowers
still on the bough, now creased as satin;
and how I felt a separation so complete
that there at the threshold of the cave
I could look back and see the shadow of my name
holding hard to the shadow of my old life –

while outside something private conjured itself:
snow plains, white, crisp northerliness – and elk
in a long group leaving hoof-prints
that go four inches deep. Condensation
flowering in the long call of their breath.
All the answers of the spirit can be found
in an animal beginning its rest. Their front legs
bending, like the leading part kneeling down at a step –
the back legs hesitating, like that other nature
that is unsure and wavering and doubts
but for a moment kneels down in togetherness.

Listening to the Accent of Borges

(for D.)

A green branch shakes as each vowel's spoken;
their magnificent fraying is pronounced.
His burred, curled saying – as if it's dissolving
into white smoke on the fire of his breath;

I knew another man who worked the boats
who spoke like this; he had cracked hands
and a sharp eye; he had the speaker's voice,
like cool rains stirring through burnt roses.

Houdini

I would have come across the water
to have seen you dressed
in the stiff jewellery of irons,
the cold and zero-ed chainlink,
wearing the sigil of the padlock
and swallowing its key.

Watching the platform gather lights,
I would have liked to know:
your hands, what do they call themselves:
rescuer or rescued,
as blood is felt in those far stations
of the skin, again.

It seems important, maybe more
for us who stand and watch.
Should we only see the second part,
the freeing act of love;
or should we count the first part, too:
when these hands set the locks.

Beginnings

Let us begin with the sea and the naming of things:
below the window, just slightly more than a stone's throw away,
is the water and the nearby *Seal Grounds*,
and past this, *The Gull Fields* –
meaning the wet blue pasture that the birds dive in.

In *Beowulf* they called the sea, *The Whale Road* –
the name for the waves between the islands,
for the black seaweed like a fringe of oil seeping
from the rocks around the coast.

Here, the name for our stretch of ocean is: *The Sound*.
The Sound, we say – coming from the Norse word *Sund* –
meaning a narrow stretch of water that can be swum.

And I like *The Sound* as its best name,
since it opens up the chance to ask:
who is working on *The Sound* today?
Whose hands are dipping in *The Sound*?
Which fishermen?
And what are they dragging up from *The Sound*?

Sitting here, so much comes back to the sea and to names.
The names – from memory – of the good boats
that would travel across the earliest window:
The Kintra Lass, The Huba, The Very Likely.
We knew these boats and their families.

We had the name of solid things – of the hill
that shelters the bay being *Maraval* –
Norse again – *Hill of the Horses.*

Which brings me, lastly, to the name for this whole place.
This view – let us give it a name, something new-old:
Seat Past Which the Storms Come in; Song's Harbour.
Let us call it: *Place of Cool Sun; Rain's Last Outpost; First Home.*

Island Sonnets: The Poem

The island of the poem finds its map.
Rising, inked, as a solitary cliff, sheet white
as if from the earliest, purest seams of chalk.

Along footholds borne in the rock
the sad bird, Meaning, calls from its nest,
beyond decipherment. On its windswept meadow,

the vowel of the stone wall meets
the vowel of the burdock, and they dance.
First of the heart's landfalls, last

sanctuary of voles and spittle-wheat.
Place, as in childhood, where the music
of the wind whistles at the window of the one house.

Landing here, even once, is to find yourself
shaken into being.
                         Or, so we imagine.

The Burning of the Bridge

Look how the girder blazes on its arch;
the steel meridian, the central walk,
lights up between two darknesses: the deep,

the deep reflected in the night. Each cross-beam
burns into a tender X, as their two landscapes
understand, too late, their brightening gulf.

These later times, I pour our strongest drop,
a twenty year, more kerosene than drink,
three turns of pure fire in a tumblered glass;

this way, we share the spirit of the drink:
she tastes, I taste. Each mouth swirls round its flame
before, between night's coasts, they meet and kiss.

After the Ending of the World

Most likely it will be the ants,
but if I could decide who takes our place
I choose the birds,

building their gathered parliament,
housing their heaven
in the unfathomable out-of-reach,

which for them would be the deep earth;
perhaps they would hold
to the ripe, sure, divinity of soil,

to mud dark spring – with the one hope
to someday see the veil lift,
a veil, as is right, of moss and wet timothy.

First Fires

This one skill keeps: an artistry with fires:
feeling the sure cast-iron start,
the spreading of the kindling,
the island of the log's true place.

Older, my parents would give me the choice:
on Sundays, I could come to mass
or stay at home, heretical,
to warm the house for their coming back –

ash-drawer billowing as it was untipped,
it smoked like grace; hands smudged like Pentecost.
Winter's room and its setting pact,
it wasn't heat and wasn't light

and wasn't something I understood,
but now I see what drew my body down:
parents kneeling in their church,
I, too, was kneeling by the grate.

Young man tending the young fire
of his life. That pale first-smoke winding
the up-river of the chimney-breast.
I stoked this flame in the empty house.

From the Devil's Songbook

To those in darkness, a bag of dark;
to the thirsty mouths, give sand in brimming cups;
bring the lonely to their locking room
and slam it shut – bring the bear to the trap;

bring the grieving another absence –
and never let it talk; bring wounds
a second knife; bring scissors to the knot –
bring anger – these days, it's what serves us best.

Love Letters from the Tenth Year of Marriage

Dear

and, maybe, summer finds us there again:
river-green France. Home of a last holiday
where it was just us. Coupled. Though not quite.
Him, stowaway in his three-month womb.
How worried we were. I lugged the suitcase
past the horse fields. You walked beside,
path through the shade, divine in a sundress.
More than halfway to responsible,
but still part-way to romance, we lived
that small life of love. The glass-framed bay-doors
of the balcony wide open.
                        One evening,
preparing for something I now forget,
you stepped out naked of the bathroom, stomach
looking for all life like a porch-bulb in the fog
the contours hazing, and this whisper of
emitting just slightly passed itself. My god,
everything changed. To waiters I said thank you
not once but in both languages – for safety
or luck or just in thanks. Love, let's return,
as if, all told, there's such a going back.

Island Sonnets: Mingulay

A bowman's paradise,
the bird-cliff holds
a million feathers
for their flights.

The two-hour boat.
Our furthest south.
The shearwaters lift
above the brink,
and then above that.

Here, you pull ashore
way past the mark.
Not where the bow
was tilted up
but where the arrow landed.

The Egg Gatherers of St Kilda

Climbers, holding to their cliff-face,
they took the downward path, the rock-cut
and notch-sure route. Hard-skinned and calloused,
they held against the wind's salt push.

Egg-gathering. Hung from their mid-shelf's
continent above the wave-crash,
they reached between the bird and nest
for a palm of warmth. Shelled, fragile theft;

life went in uproar against life,
as the egg bag filled, the grip kept.
For them, wild balance was the work.
I have been told I share this blood.

The End of Heaven

(after Hassan-i-Sabbah)

In 1092 –
> heaven grew ripe there:
that secret garden in Alamut,
near desert mountains, North Iran.

Small paradise of brass-jugged wine,
figs in green skin. New acolytes,
drugged, were brought inside the walls

and told that they had died – that this,
the soft new bed, the cup and maid
and choir, was what their faith had earned.

Imagine them, confused and saved,
drinking eternity's well water,
finding its dates both sweet and hard.

*

Death would last for three days, a short summer,
then, drugged again, they'd wake outside
the walls being told: a miracle

had whispered breath back in their bodies.
But if they wanted back to heaven
then all they had to do was serve.

*

I think of them, these quiet souls,
sleepless surely, with what must yawn
in them. That first night in the camp,

renewed, returned to the hard ground
and all its skyline. A new soul
is needed for each new life.

Who hasn't known this unwillingness:
that first self waving from its cliff-edge
to where the newer self sits waiting,
dumb, unsure, on its readied earth.

On the Deep Ocean

(after Laforgue)

Again, the night's come, full and clear,
quietly infinite – and no one's
making a sound beneath our moon;

let nothingness come, pale and ready,
let it be both the eucharist
and the high altar; the guiding arm

and this whole unknowable – let
it be the only word that holds
inside the language…

                        Far from all

the prattle and outcry that's going on,
far from meaning, far from hurt
and those with longing in their bones,

I watch this one star come rising out –
where rising is a type of speech,
addressed to this whole vastness, which

the vastness doesn't hear. And this
is fine. No – no, this is good.

Mouse

There's not much room in literature for the mouse;
though, door flung open, sometimes it creeps in,
like Dickinson when she says, 'Grief is a Mouse' –
and it sits there by her sleeve, a few inches
of shyness, brown furred, desolate as a grass stem.

Of course, Burns gifted his own mouse a field
just as it was cropped, scythed, bound. The grain folded
into sheaves. Mouse, it did not gain much
and you can see it darting, in the end,
to the snow-like wild fringes of the margin.

Rats, though. Rats are everywhere in books.
They chew through Hamelin, and in Camus's *The Plague*
they're set like death's black letters on the house-steps.
Heaney has them run across the ponds,
Christs of the sewer-pipe, always in trespass.

Not so the mouse. Now reading, I look to turn
the page and discover him twitching and gnawing
the print line, the grained lettering. A symbol
of quiet, soft, dignified life: the rare
and seldom. Startled, startling – then gone.

Dear,

The train's now sliding from Aberdour,
still empty, just three others
travelling through the June's pandemic,
sunlight on the North Sea;
I've been thinking of those early letters
we found at the back of the drawer:
I had been in Nepal and you had been working
in the gallery in the park,
the exhibitions of scientific drawings.
We hadn't been together more than six months,
but reading them, we seemed unwell with love,
marking every word, absolutely;
it hurt me, can I say this, to read them,
they read like the love of two other people –
and yes, maybe it shamed me, too,
since it seemed a love I am incapable of:
drunk and in the blood –
which is why I want to write to you
shaming the next version of me.
I do love you – maybe not in a wildness
unless it is the wildness of stone and stream,
wild in the closeness – a man, greying,
but thinking of you, as the carriage shakes
somewhere between Kinghorn and Kirkcaldy.

Rosemary

Out on the pavement,
I thought of St Augustine and his pears –
those green leaves swaying in the heat,
midsummer, their ripening point;

his need just the need of a hand
with nothing in it. And so he picked,
filling the basin of his shirt.
I can't remember, did he eat

even one or throw them all out;
the theft being enough, and too much.
Casting the yellow-skinned flushed pears,
to pray with their juice on his hands.

* * *

Which is to say,
one evening, when it was dark enough,
I went and stole the rosemary
from a neighbour's garden. Their lights on,

the bodies tucked inside the glow
behind the curtains, behind the glass.
What was the same: that something steered
me on my course. And what was different:

that I enjoyed it, took and kept
the herb – also, I wrote the poem
and not a prayer. Which is not
that different, but not quite the same.

On the Bone Oracles

– shoulder bone was best for it.
Flat and long, bound where their necks flex,
whisper distance to the plough-strap,

with knowledge of the field pull and weight –
and, cut clean out, both pale and even
as an open book; you wrote the future onto it.

Such a dream: writing onto calcium;
the bone's carved-free dust blown away softly
by the close-by mouth. The act

to see inside the mind of heaven
as though it were a room with a peephole
and god were there, talking to himself.

Sometimes, when we write, we should think of this.

Wildness

All things grow quiet, even the wild horses
bowing near the church field;

I've seen them change, rain clouds in the distance
as they home in towards shelter:

a barn-side, a stone wall, the dip of a hill.
It's the same when a stray dog comes,

they stand like painters in a field
softly waiting for a thing to happen:

the grass to move, owner to call it home;
some mid-point between dignity and panic,

they bend, listening to the wind speaking;
silent, neither in agreement nor disagreement.

Lighthouse Keeper, Doubt

This isn't much. The short beam travels
Cantrick Head, Holy Isle, Cape Wrath.
There is no path, just the beam turning
its hundred-metre, lit circumference.
What keeps me here? The sudden weather
striking against the staggered column.
Waves hit and I hear: *beauty* – then a pause
then *beauty*, this patterfall of rain,
like barley dropping on a drumskin,
the sea's wide roar – the scent of rocks
sprayed with salt water. Nothing's averted.
No person's brought to some saved home.
But even were I steering a beam of darkness
along an unlit stretch, I'd serve this sound.

Island Sonnets: The Shadow

Back home – brought in to see his body
we saw his shadow lying next to him,
stretched out, his own dark sentry sleeping,
at last allowed to sleep, since the full ruin
already swept the town. It took his profile
to the 9W glow of the bedside lighting
and copied him – brother and own dark twin.

Maybe I see too much of love in everything
but with the candles flaring in the room,
we stood alone but saw his shadow, grieving,
flinging itself down on the road of the bed,
laying out – private, quiet, loving –
it would miss him like itself. This still-black coal
beside the coal now ash-pale from its burning.

What is the Poem?

What is the poem?
Just the soul singing in its box.

And if there is no soul?
Then it's just the box singing.
Bearing out its emptiness.

Dear,

wanting to picture you smiling,
shaking you head at the comparison,
let me say this: that our marriage, now,
has lasted as long as The Trojan War.
Ten years since leaving the wedding car
just as the lightning storm opened,
and you carried, and then I carried,
the white handfuls of your bridal train
to save it from the wet ground.
Do you know, speaking of the war,
my favourite part was the small detail
in Aeschylus: *Ida to the Hermaean crag in Lemnos*
to the mighty blaze upon the island succeeded,
third the summit of Athos sacred to Zeus.
This way, the beacons lit from Troy
to Greece, bringing the message home
that the war was done;
and just think, for ten years some had to wait,
oil barrel and wood pyre,
watching for the light that was the signal.
And surely, if you think of it,
just as likely a man and woman,
or else a small family,
were sent onto one of those snow mountains,
far from the war, far from great actions.
There, far from the battle cry and the field,
I picture the other quiet duties:

food gathering, frost clearing
and picture, too, the decade of evenings,
small petal beside small petal.
Darling, there's a quietness to love now
which these letters go with and go against,
but can you see them, the small human outlines
moving across Lemnos or Athos,
the snow in the tree-line's forest,
the cabin. The hope that the war ends,
the second hope, that no word or light
or blazing hill-top fire is ever seen.

Blackbird Psalm

Come to me, blackbird of the garden.
Berry-eater with the yellow beak,
draw close to me, unsinging man
on the unsinging step of grey stone.

Black tongue of the world's mouth, show me
the moving and the stillness on the branch.
Teach me, how a life just one-tenth song
and nine-tenths not, sets the grass singing.

The Transformed Fight

The car park has its own epiphanies,
come closing time, a large crowd listening

past the breaking sorrows of the night.
I'll knock the living daylights out of you.

A phrase, we find, replacing blood with light,
as though there in the words before the start,

the slyest act of tenderness. Two men
go swaying, like new candles in a church,

acknowledging the late-May radiance
that's even in this other man they hate.

I never heard of kindness stretch to this.
Both, a spring window – that they try to reach.

The Windows

...it was all hutch and hatch...

SEAMUS HEANEY

When those new windows, sashed and cased, were hoisted in,
later than most I understood the phrase 'as clear as glass'.
Out went those wrinkled ancient fingerprints of panes;
fogged, misted, smudged by time, or else holding a little breath
of a ripple through their ice. All these years I didn't know
I wasn't seeing clearly. But now, if asked to make my stand
I'd say that love comes with seeing things just as they are –
clear detailed laburnum in September's garden, crisply swaying.
First among the miracles was the laying hands on the blind.

The Nine Billion Names

Tonight, I recall the translations of these hills:
Easaval, *Hill of the Waterfall,*
Beinn Sciathain, *Mountain of Scree,*
and place my foot on the slope of each name,

knowing once, I swam the *Green-Water Loch,*
stripping at the bank, wading my name
into the duck-reeds and swaying algae – and felt
the greenness swimming next to me.

At times, too, naming has brought me close to shame.
Stepping out with my son into the torchlight's
open countryside. Wide-fields of midnight,
rich and almost harvestable, and, pointing up
reciting: *The Swan, The Plough, Orion's Belt*
then pulling him along to hide
that I only have the three names for the stars' shapes
and all the rest is spread and lit and blank.

Arthur C. Clarke has a tale of monks unravelling
what they saw as the nine-billion names of God,
and I see them, the colour of their robes
named *turmeric* or *yolk* or *dawn,*
a vibrant yellow brought over the bare skin,
as they wake in the cloistered cell
and see, perhaps, the woodlouse on the cobbles,
like a ridged carriage, a grey horse-less caravan,
finding a name there: *God, the tired foot lifting*
on the stone road.
                        Their cosmic, serious labour,
watching for the name revealed by the dog

sleeping near the thrush nest, the cricket leaping
itself and its name into the named air.
Discovery after discovery adds to the name-hoard.

So, Sunday morning streams through Sunday's window,
the yawn of the pink foxgloves in the yard.
My wife's feet stirring the sun's dust on the floor.
I call her, marvelling that when we met
she had one name – but now, there are any one
of twenty names that I could put to her.
The personal, the intricate, these variances
of privateness. Our treasury of naming.

Our life's book fills with the street names,
the job titles that we took on through our time,
the shop fronts, the book spines with full lettering,
alongside these parts of her. I jar the name
of the window so the name of the breeze pours in,
and I am with those monks on their mountain, saying:

this much I understand of things:
a great part will be revealed by watching
but the greater part will be revealed by love.

The Sound

Be not afeard; the isle is full of noises

Caliban, *The Tempest*

Listen: footsteps under moonlight.
You left the echoing road, the verge blanket of the grass
to now walk just on sand, each footstep saying *hush*
as if to the one previous. *Hush. Hush.* The beach path
all feldspar and dusted quartz. *Hush. Hush.*
The razorshell. The conicals of whelks.

Alone, passing the snores of driftwood hunkered
on the beach silk – you might hear the something else
that isn't the sea returning to the beach,
or the corncrake in the small blacked-out cathedral
of collected thatch; that isn't the lighthouse
making the one sound of its light;

autumn coming in on the black Atlantic,
you hear your pulse responding to the frost,
singing, like a second bird, from the gardens
of your neck and wrist and breast. Its *lub-dup*
as a pity-tune, now a mating track, now
the last call of the dodo or the great auk;

all the disappearing sounds of the world come back,
here, beneath the percussion of the starlight
and the rustle in the grasses. And the thought occurs,
surprising you, of a bow-hand weaving in the lateness –
the high strings of the wanderer's porchlight,
the low strings of the stopped life on its path.

ACKNOWLEDGEMENTS

Thanks are due to a great number of people – but special gratitude to Ian, Michael and John, and to the patient members of the Fife Writers Group.

Thank you, too, to the editors of *The Dark Horse*, *The Poetry Review*, *Bad Lilies*, *The London Magazine*, *Gutter Shenandoah* and *Nimrod Journal*, where a number of these poems were first published.

The epigraph from *The Conference of the Birds* by Farid ud-din Attar is from Dick Davis's translation in *Love in another Language: Collected Poems and Selected Translations* (Carcanet, 2017).

Lastly, special mention to Neil at Bloodaxe for supporting this book – and to Soren and Catriona for being the best of people.

Niall Campbell was born in 1984 on the island of South Uist, one of the Outer Hebrides of Scotland. He received an Eric Gregory Award in 2011 and an Arvon-Jerwood Mentorship in 2013, and won the *Poetry London* Competition in 2013. His debut pamphlet, *After the Creel* Fleet, was published by Happenstance Press in 2012. His first book-length collection, *Moontide* (Bloodaxe Books, 2014), won what was then Britain's biggest poetry prize, the £20,000 Edwin Morgan Poetry Award, as well as the Saltire First Book of the Year Award; it was also shortlisted for the Forward Prize for Best First Collection, the Fenton Aldeburgh First Collection Prize and the Michael Murphy Memorial Prize, and is a Poetry Book Society Recommendation. *First Nights: poems*, a selection from *Moontide* with additional new poems, was published by Princeton University Press in the US in 2016. His second book-length collection, *Noctuary* (Bloodaxe Books, 2019), was shortlisted for the 2019 Forward Prize for Best Collection. He wrote the libretto for *Draught*, an opera by Anna Appleby, which was performed by the BBC Philharmonic in 2022. His third collection, *The Island in the Sound*, was published by Bloodaxe in 2024. He now lives in Fife.